ANYTIME BLUES

poems by

LINDA LERNER

Some of these poems have/will appear in the following journals:

THE LUCID STONE; HOME PLANET NEWS; SPEAK EASY PRESS; POEMS THAT THUMP IN THE DARK; GRAFFITI RAG; MAIN STREET RAG; BROUHAHA; AX FACTORY REVIEW; HALF TONES TO JUBILEE; SLUG FEST.LTD.; PUDDING; BOUILLABAISSE; HOUSE ORGAN; BULL-HEAD; MEDICINAL PURPOSES; MEAT WHISTLE QUARTERLY; THE CAFE REVIEW; ONE TRICK PONY;JAZZ TRADITION(anthology—PIG IRON PRESS); MEDICINAL PURPOSES; BARD (Re-Presst Publishing Co.); WISEWOMEN¹S WEB (internet); LIES PEOPLE TELL (INTERNET); NEXUS; CAPRICE

First Edition.

ANYTIMEBLUES

P.O. Box 8328
New Haven, CT 06530

www.webcom.com
yeolde@mail.ntplx.net

ISBN: 1-889289-36-1
Printed in the USA by Morris Publishing
3212 E. Hwy 30
Kearney, NE 68847

For Tony

Brought together by one who
*had **IT** absolutely*
*made sure I got **IT***
Yeah "a joyful noise..."

We keep it alive

“The Journey is only from there to there to there”
—*Anonymous Bronx Sage*

“Slowly I Realized
The Best Way To
Hold on,
Was to just
Let Go”
(Graffiti found—from 24.7 Artzine)

TABLE OF CONTENTS

I.

CITYNOISE

when big woman opens her mouth
on the subway   the picket line   in
      the classroom   when she
      opens her mouth anyplace
            it's new york
train screeching off language
   sanitation truck pick up
      street drilling in
        a brain's eardrum
when big woman opens her mouth
                    injustice
                              hurling
                                      out
                              of control
bullies a city: under siege: under cover...
big woman trapped inside
hears nothing: nothing from those
she lives with/passes on the street
            every day   nothing
about her pain
            she can word
sculpt visible for eyes
to hear   nothing
that can be shouted
                          over the noise...

BLIZZARD '96

saw a man talking to a pigeon
in from of Blimpies
over 20 inches of snow fallen
he looks the pigeon straight in the eye,

    "you & me got a problem,"

grey stubble on bloated reddish skin
dirty cup of coffee in his hand
and deep in record-breaking pristine white
                softening new york harshness...

    "where we gonna get us some food?"

Fairytalecity   no cars   trucks
people acting so nice
and this man nobody sees...
  want to tell him
i know about hunger-worry too
                        but how
on a full stomach
able to buy all the food i want
tell him how difficult it is
to find a few seeds
my man gone to some bottom
vanished like all the seeds
                        how to
make my voice heard
    thru all this snow

WHAT DO I SEE WHEN I SEE

Old man stares into his cup of black coffee,
black even after he drinks it;
                    see him
in McDonald's window, well dressed
crouching in his trench hole-dark
                    late afternoons
on Court street
                    on my way to/this detour
                                        then
back to old turf: hunting
for job/apartment, life in rougher
                              90's climate/
whining from bones/joints...
Odd time for love to crocus;
                                  feel
urge to hit the sky-road
ignore the economics of breathing..
                                  see
back-packing angels taking flight,
no planes, miles in the air
smoking cigarettes, having drinks
thumbing their noses at everyone
more frightened of unemployment than death
                                        who
don't see that old man
                          never will,
perfect flying weather, and...

          "Hey lady, watch where
          you're going..."

                          Big Mac/breaks
inches from me...blinding gasoline sun,
angry 5 o'clock stampede; horns jazz
                                        murder improv,
someone's shoe nipping my heel
screams, "bitch, watch where..."

And I don't know where
                              on Court street

March, 1995

SUBWAY JAM

Pre xmass crowds no. 2 IRT/stalling
starts $1.50 grumble
everyone's bass free session...

wouldn't mind if service improved
no crime beggars...

where you gonna put them,
New Jersey? Tried that.

Starts/stalls

$1.50 yeah

Whole house in Wisconsin cost $ 7. 000...

Six months rent for
a studio here...

yeah

head bopping trane in full swing
now everyone's miles duke
edged for their turn...
Mine? buried in
Chicago snow so high a voice
sleighs right out the attic window
blasted by ex serviceman's first
visit back in thirty years
robbed at ATM machine
skidding on airport runway

caught up in a city's melodyrhythm
stalls/starts
$1.50 rams/MY STOP:
mutes "a joyful noise"

AROUND & AROUND I GO

always a broadway
even in alcatraz
and washington square
shrunk in north beach/
greenwich village place where
i once sat with a boy
playing his girl so sweetly...
names geograph me
names like bones
my own street name
jumping out at me in SF/mission
block i fell in love with
before i knew
                    falling
ahead of myself in the dark...
up concrete hills
i climb back   back
boston's gentler slopes
fleshed in a motel bed
marriage proposal/vow
my body took
before **yes** escaped
and i grasped forever
means how much/not
how long/and
just how long that is

around & around i go...

union square greenwich

                    the battery

NY in SF/anyplace: home

ESPECIALLY THOSE EMPTY STREETS

those new jersey towns
woodbridge   cranford   metuchen
big houses   empty streets
bug me...
walk blocks   no one
to ask directions...
a few 50's wedding gowns
clothes in shop windows
no red ribbons protesting aids
no graffiti anger climbing walls
rap gunning out of cars...
six figure husbands leave
at dawn for wall street   world
trade center offices
back after dark...empty
rooms in those houses
bug me too
like those set dining room tables
perfectly folded napkins
no crumbs
no crumbs ever...

this is pre 60's wired to the 90's
computers   cell phones
lots of pink   cookie jars   sweet
home nick nacks   plump wives
who've put in hours outside...
 jobs   classes   lovers
comes down to shopping
in the end...

newsprint murders   crimes
no blood / cops waving sticks
beating innocent / people
crying injustice...only now and then
someone rushing from
car to house to car
whose body talk says *no...*

this body wants to feel
a voice banging into it
fumbling *sorry*
misses the *hey fuck off....watch where*
you're going shoving/pushing
new york argument to get thru/win
a visible *nobody who'll help you*
like crane and hardy's yearned for
temple to fling bricks at
god to curse out/and i have...

but this is new jersey not the universe
woodbridge cranford metuchin
pretty towns
big houses
empty streets

damn those empty streets

WHEN AN EDITOR PRAISING MY POEMS ASKS *BUT WHY* & DO YOU HAVE ANY THAT *ARE MORE*

what can I tell her
this is New York not Oregon
my metro card only takes me
so far most of it underground:
Brooklyn Manhattan Bronx/
thru conductor's
announcements of police action
meeting people so programmed
they don't even know
kids warring up for the day
pushing: death god music
off track rhythms
my poems pick up &
grabbed an editor out west
if only i'd discard
the *bummed out...dead lives...*
the *desolation*
couldn't see the rhythm
is the sound of the image &
can't be separated
as i from this city...
underground
where i choose to live
my poems are born
& real is a pain
in the butt nagging me
for spare anything my
space...REAL
underground because
sometimes a guy pulls out
a horn & blows
on a street in blazing sun
he's underground blowing
& it's that sunflower
Ginsberg saw by some dirty railroad tracks
full of a city's industrial grime
golden inside
unmistakable/
sunflower

MR. TAMBOURINE MAN PLAYING AT PRINCESS DIANA'S FUNERAL

A sixties hangover wild Garcia hair & beard
strumming with dirty fingers around Washington Square fountain
backup radioed: death long distance / death close up
and old defiance in the air: smells right/exactly right...
this isn't my time except it is;
as much out of step now as then
as much in step as i'll ever be
seek out places hot with language color
hot seasons crowds once shunned...
no good without burnt hamburger smells
nicotine air to breathe memory:
when now was immortality...
mr. tambourine man strumming
fire thru the *arctic* what
a woman did with a clandestine smile those eyes
fire thru the *arctic*...
mr. tambourine man strumming
from his gut: what's good for you will kill you
to stop is to die
strumming *this moment* so loud
no other sound
for the crowd swarming around their princess
around mr. tambourine man
around a fountain of youth:
no other sound

Saturday, September 6, 1997

BLUESPOET

For Tony Moffeit
(who never writes on black ice)

bluespoet is riding
in his car riding the sound
of the road   of a jazz horn
the pen riding urges
in his blood his genes
riding blind with sight
down colorado mountains
    riding his vision
thru boundary semantic
    of living & dead
riding the umbilical cord
    back to his mother
    to the ghost of himself
riding his own death
frees himself of it
        on a mountain pass
in colorado his car spinning
on black ice on a word
                        a line
        spinning
                off
        anytimeblues
into a ravine
song
drumming
life back
bluespoet must ride to breathe
cut up bleeding
bluespoet gets back in his car
to saddle america
tapping secret energies
of the earth heals himself
miles of mississippi delta
backroads   and always marguerita
in the "honky tonk wind" marguerita
in the rain & snow
marguerita filling his head

crazy rhythms driving his pen
across the sangre de cristo mountains
        into mystery & danger
riding a train's whistle
wolf howl moan of a voodoo woman
riding a love supreme
to new orleans
    bluespoet is riding
        he's riding

OUT

the breath

CRASHING AT HERBIE HANCOCK CONCERT/ WASHINGTON SQUARE PARK

8/26/96

came to catch a whiff of his sound
in shorts and long dresses
purple hair   ringed noses
anything that wasn't   everybody
                    came to see
the man who made the sound
as i did last year when
roy hargrove steered high

just thrown off love
further than i ever knew down existed

same woman happened to sit beside me
                didn't recall
and i who am not that i anymore
                didn't remind her...

packs of solitaries   couples
on benches/backs   on grass
hanging from bleaches
good rough edged feel to late summer
        dead-nosed cops
knowing better than to breathe deeply
recall prohibition/excitement   years
sneaking / back   end of century...

came with instruments/books
            blankets/food
with their own buzz
music crashed thru...relentless sax
quartet lost in blasting improv
soared by   and
the crowd jumped on...

closed my eyes and
held on to the sound
riding past the woman i was
                              and am
barely seeing the man
who took us on this ride...
when it ended
and the woman who didn't remember me
                                          said good bye
i had long gone

II.

SUDDENLY MOUNTAINS

looked up and saw mountains
wide band of shaded blue then white
                    and I'm still
walking down same New York brownstone street
mountains like I saw in New Mexico last year
            still January morning, 1996
same Korean fruit stand
nannies wheeling baby carriages
familiar strangers   but here is not
                    where I just was
                    missing my lover
with me all year in absence
wondering how he'll find this place
                    so far out-
                    west in Brooklyn
            no train station   bus stop
and still walking down this mountained street
feeling better than I have in a long time
swear I could hear fast horse
                                riding pursuit

NEW AGE

generation X huddled
outside saint anything college
        smoking war
pierced eyebrows noses ears
flesh screaming stigmata
and mona lisa smiles...

head bowed kneeling elders
        don't get it
around nipples   clits
                        must hurt...

outside saint anything college
tongues ringed voiceless...

something more than fashion or art
more than they'll ever grasp
few feel again...

like **their** madonna dangle crosses
from wrists   necks   for sport
wound themselves before
someone else does it...

seen parents crawling to priests
        landlords   bosses   husbands
crouching behind locked doors/barred windows
        who've never been alive
        fear being murdered
whispering prayers for a child
        boarding a plane   a life
        who've never flown
        fear crashing

generation X hears their eyes asking
        does it hurt
          does it hurt to live

WHEN THE HOLY MAN CAME

Could have been a rock concert
        heavy metal, grunge
resurrected Elvis,   Lennon
Garcia, newly dead, no one quite believed...
                        tight security, but
black garbed adoration
            crashed sexual boundaries,
                        incense speeding heads
                                            back...
Woodstock / Beatle generation
screaming voice out of throat
            could have been
Rolling Stones' second coming
        Mick performing live
            miracle
sparking a crowd's orgasm.
Been an atheist long as I recall
but recognized the fervor:
When my lover looked into
my eyes when he touched and lifted me
                        holy...holy...

BREAKOUT

and thru punctuation roadblock/stopsigns
knocking down capital ridiculousness
running on what couldn't be confiscated
because learned freedom from love
    I couldn't **not** anymore
                march 1996
ran into the virtual streets
i've walked all my life
    cycling down pages

    lovemaking riding
    without breaks a helmet

same smart assed brooklyn kid bucking authority
painted lips bright lust
out with some innocent boy
in full glare of parental anger

now riding on the beat of breath only

        riding fast

                for my life

HITCHING TO THE MILLENNIUM

nature's chick wouldn't deal
money   business: anything technology
what wasn't   now
meant family tie-me-downs
burial plot her mother gifted
jumped academia to think
with her nerves

in the name of death disguised
nature's chick
child of the 60's kicked
too hard   too well...
90's vagabond   street lady now
with shelter   food   and no home
wandered into cyber country...
tired needing to unload
found a vacant computer
and created a website...
a few decades baggage
                                        it felt good
                                        real good...
crashing on a line of leonard cohen's
            "...you've touched her perfect body
                        with your mind"
she dreamed of one she loved
                                        long gone
                                        she hoped to save...
if mind was body after death
she may have found a way to freeze/preserve

landlord returned confiscated/shutdown
meant back to the streets   a squatter
meant new underground
plenty of transients like her
to share computer digs...
trouble was those damn viruses

highway tricksters
not enough space
and always on the run...
been there

nature's chick
child of the 60's
back on the road
thumbing a ride

DON'T GIVE ME THAT EX BULLSHIT

i lived inside a man
lived in me...
lost in vodka waters and
now just lost

                                        but sometimes
one of those late afternoons something
about the light
alone hours his
"once given can't be taken back"
                                        choking me

and i know
there's no ex anything...
it's all sea again
i'm diving down
riding our horse off the edge...
sometimes i'm speaking to a crowd
even thinking/ worries
his voice in me
          outloud
i'm like that star trek woman
who's everyone she's ever loved...
i look at it this way:
like a plot of immortality
          undermining deaths

HAS THE MAGIC

Ok Irish,
you can pull a tale from a penny
make words snake charms
numb their poisoned sting.
Listeners' ears rise
to your need's pitch/theirs now:
percussion pulse set heard
in your after hour dark.
Yes, blue sun if you see it.

But Irish,
there's a witch-woman doesn't
need your potions; walks
invisible high wires to you
where you can't get to
x-rays thru
leaves her prints on your nerves forever
makes you feel
wind/rain/sun/in her oceans.
Watch her: pours coffee...
Feel the wind licking your skin?
Watch her move.
Air thickens: woods lush with fable.

PRE BIRTHDAY RAMBLIN BLUES

i sit by the east river
        all the steel
glass power   new york
                        corners

come here to refuel
        when there's
nothing
fish out of these muddy waters
        draw from the sun
all eye   i am all eye...

tiny hords begging cans
        on piers below
and beggar myself
recall what it is
for a man to love me
to pain and be
grateful there's that...

kids training to hurt
fly after pigeons and
how cute   parents follow proud...

tanned young middle age
        in tight shorts
walking with his dog
stops near my bench
to do push ups

two of the beautiful people
        by the railing
        wall street suit
        mini skirt/ black shades

golden his long pony tail
golden her shoulder length hair

hold bagged bud and light up
        to a shrine
        floating nowhere
        across the river...

sun in my eye
doesn't stop me from seeing

                beggarwoman
dragging the river
                    miraging
man who gave me second birth

my head in his lap
i recall looking up
        into his eyes

        sky

it was everywhere
nothing more
i wanted

III.

MY MOTHER'S DIGS

place jam packed: pronouns from
86 years come to crash
guy in knickers/dead now
bossing her around   could be
father or brother   acting like
smart assed bank manager this morning...
and the younger man who's
hurt her with another woman
            "that's it
            we're thru" cry
rising out of a dead girlhood
a mother's cry
from her breasts/womb...
names i want names
she hesitates   and
does it really matter
father   husband   son
                        who
murdered a woman's soul
                        who
looks down at this
poor immigrant's wife/widow
                        which
young fool   doctor/son
only wants her money
            lent 'em plenty
            in the depression
            never came back...
who ma   i shout futilely
sometimes to still me
she throws out a name
we both know it
isn't
and is...ghost
that haunts her/ghost she is

INTO THE CRADLES THEY GO

grandparents middle aged   young
irish jewish italian   crying
in poems dragged to bars   coffee houses

oh father/mother who art in heaven

across america

forgive us
we knew not what we did...

runaways pilgrimaging back:
old williamsberg brooklyn   a father's birth-
place left forever   holy sanctuary
holy the heavy oak furniture/inherited
coffins a life now   holy
every blanket   piece of linen
holy parents in their after-death years...

he would have been there

daughter's cry

on that line protesting with me

who never did before...

and i who am not them   would never return
journey thru poems to a man
lost   good as dead   to
every bar-face flushed vodka high   to
a lover with a father's
hands woke a woman's body...

the poets are crying in their cradles
bars   coffee houses   anywhere allowed:
holy   all that isn't anymore

IF THIS AIN'T A JAZZ FUNERAL
I DON'T KNOW WHAT IS

(anniversary—6/21/97)

stuck in o'brien   t-shirt traffic
two days   outside
moffeit's   voodoo speakeasy
    swimming thru bourbon's muddy
brass wind blowing premonitions...

hey tony, where's chickenman
selling gris bags these days?

thru pirates alley & hot sax to
cool off on steam
                    boat down the mississippi/
crash in hurricane...

eyes opening blue
upbeat zydeco   all night blues...
mayfield   ruffins swinging thru
donna's bar & grill
fling me new orleans high...

forget chickenman
rafting thru alligator hungry   swamps
old plantation ghosts...

drum pounding flood:
dead housed above
ground threatening to

trumpet blasts evacuation:
                              home/

death certificate waiting... my
love reminding me he's *still*
        intending to *stay*
                    dead...

third time bury
rest of his tangible remains
my body sweating jazz / every orifice
eyes ears cunt he
couldn't get enough of...
third time: *last/final*

hot hot improv rites
for a nam vet survivor

ON THE VERGE OF WOMAN / AND

three girls who've never known
a boy   breaking the ice up close
giggling in the doctor's office

how many pregnancies   abortions

embarassing at their age
read marriage for miscarriage...
girl with the appointment
holds up the questionnaire
uncertain   the proper
etiquette   nobody instructed her
like her mother did about not ever
going into the garage alone with tommy
                    or any boy/alone anywhere
                                        too late now...
a woman comes out and
takes the form from her shaky hands...
                                        told to wait/
been doing that   marking time

who's getting married
                    having a baby
                                        an affair
three girls dressed up in
their mother's clothes
old smelly garments
a joke of course
no harm done
will step out of wrinkled skin
girls flirting with
the boys on the corner again
cute tommy   black hair slicked back
blue dangerous eyes
sitting in the drugstore sipping egg creams
new cardigan sweaters & pleated skirts
shiny pennies in white loafers

caught up in
their monthly cycles
promise of their birth
don't see
the cyclical turning vertical...
one bleeding again
hot angry blood
bleeding into the dumb earth...

three girls waiting
for atonement
at least explanation

CRAPSHOOT IN THE DESERT

artist enough to walk along the streets of N.Y./DC
        any time of night / on paper   confront book
        people in leather and chains   hypocrisy danger
        enough to follow the beat
and not enough   for this suburban raised mid forties man
        to get on a blind dirt road
        dirt that bites the skin
        in the eyes when the wind
        twists his vision   alone with his gut
        no job   no job waiting
        barely enough money / survives
        picks up a woman who wants
        a good fuck not a wedding ring
        conversation he could touch
        might hurt   make him scream
                blind road
                without family
                to bail him out
artist enough not to want the life he got
        returning east from
        Las Vegas/desert country   married...
        a wife whose frugality wouldn't
        permit what can happen
        that time of loneliness anyone is the one...

....

        once years back in her small hometown
        a game   passing the needle
                        the bottle
        harmless child's *pin the tall on the donkey* game/
        illness dormant for years   now
        doctors probing for cause
        when cure is remission...
        she told him all this   omitting her bad moods
        pennies counting out small portions of
        what makes life bearable if
        large enough...

not enough of an artist for this soft spoken man to
        get on **that** road
        before his soul became too tax deductible...
        but to run away when she's out
        behind her back
        speeding on his computer
        his get-a-way
           get-over

artist enough for her to have married him
        lift up her head from those
        bookkeeping margins/
        once in a while   remissions...

        like in Vegas
        the second it took them to toss/
the win

WATCH ME FLY THRU THE MOON

I am writing my clothes slowly off
to a man thousands of miles away
peeling off skins of mind
out of t-shirt and shorts
          behind literary
am writing open my buttons
          unzipping/unsnapping
to scarred flesh of soul

          does he see
          does he want to see

man who has bachelor in his blood
          "maybe some day" wishing
          after what wasn't...
I am writing my clothes slowly off
to a man this woman once was
before someone's eyes tasted
my lips on his vodka tongue
          as we talked
my clothes off in grassroots bar
          st. marks place to brooklyn
romping thru summers drunken winters/
                                        blacked out...
i am writing to a man who
will grab me anyplace
lusting more for me than a drink
writing to a blind man
          sighting my pain
 thousands of miles away

TO HELL WITH CAREFULNESS

can't be too uncareful given that loose screw
could turn up in someone's head or engine
anytime... empire state/railroad madman
crackup in the skies
not like aids real danger...
want to tell
those women with souls in ivory towers
who say *be careful*
everytime before
every before
death is careful enough...
given that loose screw balanced against
might never happen again
not ever
like on that hot june night
so hot on
st. marks/corner greenwich village
just met
could have been a serial killer/rapist
holding me
connection electrocuting on impact
any reply but yes/opening
my apartment my bedroom my cunt my soul
exploding into my life
yes
given everything: all the hell we caused
each other afterwards
yes...

FIRST TIME

Never dirtied her hands
wiping baby's shit or
taking a husband's either
head librarian of big New York university
big salary/early retirement
pension spread out
two 1950's leased apartments
first floor of brownstone
I too live in
for now. Can't afford longer.
Another back-packing university
gypsy
passing
shop-talk...
Want to say something about her
garden dying beneath my windows
my lover thinks of offering
his skills for its use
but time
he's gone, I'm looking
at apartment want ads
"I flunked my mammogram"
ashamed school girl voice
brushes past
my fumbling "sorry"
unmasking outspoken runaway
"will only take so much"
now
claws at the earth
tearing out clumps of weeds
skin blind to December cold ice-
rain blind to who's watching...
weekly deliveries/baby
pines rushed into earth
she can't get enough of
mud/dirt on her hands
face in her hair
this earth
amazing earth

I DON'T ALWAYS ANYTHING

I know a lot of dead people.
        one ph'd brain/
dead someone, scholars books;
does/says what her programmed
mind allows. On impact
classifies, categorizes...
                inherited.
Enough to secure herself
        out of breath.
Knows a lot. Not that.
When necessary, I seek her out.
Feels like jumping bail to hear,

        But you always...
        and, yesterday...

Friend, yesterday I wasn't even born:
        in this living space
        this heart, this thought.
Her good wishes, killer
threat alerts my survival instinct:
I reach for outrageous
she hasn't seen/heard...
Ah, but she's good;
        a minute, and

you're poet, that explains...

AND WITNESSING NOTHING
THAT DID NOT TAKE PLACE

so when a tenured bride in her 50th year
hankering after more *forever*
than academia or inheritance promises
asks a woman living
by her guts in permanent now
to bear witness
on this damp november first
follow her out-of- breath
walk to city hall
on the heels of the groom––
feels a stiffness in her joints/
doctors just taken the
unwanted woman out of her/
twenty-five years since divorce and
love-of-her-life expectations
maybe got scared...catching the
groom in unguarded sympathy
took his breath...
right there in city hall
rushing his inhaler on...
maybe needed to witness this skeptic
hold her peace
when a civil service voice asked
is there anyone who knows
why this couple should **not...**
explains what I was doing in
this drab waiting area
in faded blues beside
a couple dressed for a funeral as well...
when the civil service voice
said...you may now
setting off a command...
must now
i order you now
to kiss the bride...
only then...touched

WIVES OF THE LITERATI

they come to the book signing
poetry reading   memorial with
their talisman   star/cross
prayer book to heaven
plump fading women in
imaginary furs   affordable/inoffensive fur
come with their birthright   raison d'être
proud   animalmothers/these wives...
i feel the claws in their eyes
when i talk to their husbands
      to share some words
      offer my book
      my lost virginity
      my bodysoul
      signed to him
      all that i am
      MY BOOKMY BOOK
claws like knives...
the crowd salivates
cameras tearing at him
the wives smile and nod
      ok to saint him
allowed within snapshot limits
and if he lies down in
their beds once in a while
forgiven when he returns/
                        must return
she who's repository for everything HIM
all he's forgotten   lost
muse he cannot divorce
      smiles and nods
      at his rumpled excuses
more than his emissary
                  as i
more than another rival
haunting their makebelieves...
      ...smile and nod
in their imaginary furs

FOR DONALD HOCKNEY

with apologies for using your death
so shamelessly to mourn
my lost twenty-one years/
long measuring rod to slide down
& bump into a brash kid on
her way to fame a few
poems in pocket
firing ideas at you
guy who gave
the go-ahead humanities
boss/bossed no one;
philosopher in spite of a degree
whiz at anything your
mind bulls eyed...lived open door
a fast life someone said
learning of your death at 62 of lung cancer...
hell, you weren't ready
but 100% safe is dead/
if given the chance
you'd probably live the same...

didn't matter how outrageous
poets at an engineering college
creative writing classes
make it work you said
it's yours &
was for eight years...
trouble is you set a bad example
what I wouldn't find again too easily
in that world of military
adherence to rank
group minds &
Salem warnings / filtered polite
for heretics:
gave me what i now mourn...

so apologies dear friend
whose failing body made you
question the spirit's destination:
only takes someone living to home...
i didn't go to your funeral
you are not entirely dead

IV.

HALLOWEEN 1997

the dead wake from poems
i've buried them in
calling long distance
                    how far from dementia
i don't ask   a mother
calling her teen age runaway
                                        not me...
risen from the kaddish
my father hit me with
for disobedience: nobody's child/

i've earned the right:

wasn't me she bathed   fed
clothed   sent to school
even knew
                                    but sounds ok...
if i had a daughter/don't
but if i did
i'd want one like her
as wild & bad
locked up with that lover
my mother imagines me with
not stuck in this Halloween dark
alone in my skin
unprotected from ghosts/

another   born her month/day
returns now   same week as she
                                        what's happening?
back from the jazz funeral
i gave him in blood ink
death he insisted on
pulled off once more...
ghost of a mother's misaimed need
ghost of Vietnam   of himself
poet of ghosts   i wept over
& cursed   called husband:
                                        what's happening?

ANY WAY I CAN

i am writing away from
my mother's slow dying to
a book vanishing on my desk
a text easily replaced more work
marking passages not impossible
right there on my desk
a few students standing around
a Russian the last
eyeing something he couldn't afford
what my Russian born father
still reaches for
thru death thru me...
i feel it
when i visit my mother
what remains of her in the nursing home
way she pushes her plate of food
a piece of bread toward me

eat something ask your brother for a job

forgetting i'm his
daughter too a dreamer:
this isn't the bread I need
what keeps me alive...
so i understand if it's that Russian student
who took it & it's not
the book's disappearance i mind
but not seeing it happen
ever knowing for sure...
there & then gone

TO MY MOTHER IN A NURSING HOME

i bring flowers
not poems
she called *clutter* of those
zines i gave her...forgotten
in her dying/
recalled now like the love
i withheld couldn't
break thru a wall to give:
or the family
she wanted for me
not her / not only for her
i bring flowers
that don't last too long
beauty that maintains itself
not poems
wrenched from the gut
brawling too loud
for her deaf ears...
to my mother who is dying
i bring flowers
not poems

FED UP & HAVING AN ALL OUT TANTRUM

no   not another word of
someone going
out of focus   into earth to ashes
leaving my world   my soulsphere
                                        doesn't matter
it is death   not another poem

memorial: Huncke Ginsberg
                 Micheline...
the barely known colleagues
60's radical who cashed in
for a pension didn't include death
chases after his breath now in
San Diego dust...
guy half my mother's age
who should be keeping time
in a honky tonk
loosing it in a hospital room

added to the others/the closeones
3 years devastation takes its toll/
i think of the Anassazi
and wonder if it happened slow
or sudden & does it matter...

3 years   love that never
really died   said
            i am someone else now
            you do not know me
            would not care too
death that lives on...

3 years   my mother's slow motion
fall backward
Hittler's burning Jews
she whispers to me
from her hospital prison
1940's Europe she's never been in
i lied...said i was Christian

holds a finger to her lips
not a word
no   not another word

funeral   for the stillbreathing
gone: i'm declaring a moratorium
on death   any kind...

right now i'm looking out
at the Hudson...across the
world searches for
pieces of life   a Swiss plane
off Nova Scotia waters
keeping my eyes fixed on
these calm waters   on
a ship   any ship
anchored...

right now i'm leaving
my mother in the nursing home
still knows i'm her daughter
doesn't want to know more/can't
hear what she never wanted to

leaving this fragile woman
and needing that raw
disregard for   polite   proper
walk thru East Village streets
loud   w/young grunge
looking ready for war
chains   leather   pink/green
hair to defy what is still
a word   going to happen
so is love & kids...

right now is a life preserver
keeping me   the others afloat
what all the doctors
rescue missions
psychologist can't do...
right now is forever

SCIENCE FICTION TRUTH IS THE REALITY I MUST FACE

when I visit my mother
in the nursing home
wrinkled babies in carriages
unable to feed themselves
walk without falling
pushed to the point of death
back where they began...
i enter with
my estranged brother of two decades
husband & wife now
a future present
I cannot walk out of so easily;
here for our sole surviving child
for her sake   very civilized...
lawyers help us to
confiscate her life & not get caught
what she'd want
we assure outselves
for her own good
my own good
she often said
and it wasn't always   then either...
this is payback
child i wouldn't bear
orphans me
and there is nothing
i can do about it...
have no idea
what planet i am on
or how to get home/
if i'll get home

HALLOWEEN FOR REAL--NOV. 26,1998

the choice: Dracula   the devil
a nun   a pumpkin faced rabbi
the residents vote by clapping/
Dracula wins first place...
the Charleston starts up
my mother forgets
she can't   is pretending
or after 80 years on her feet
doesn't want to stand anymore
crossing her hands over bent knees
starts to show us how
she did it last night
60 years ago...

nearby teen age blue eyes
flirting thru an old woman face mask
trick or treat   trick or treat
with another patient
doesn't fool me...
someone else in knee socks & short skirt
w/ a wrinkled body suit
playing the same game
trick or treat   trick or treat...
a cad off to the side marking time
with one foot   concealing his other
making time with the singer
doesn't fool her either
w/his wheel chair & aged mask
making time like everyone here

marking time
as i am doing
before heading to a funeral home
w/my brother to pre arrange
for when   he says
just in case   i think
agnostic about death
otherwise atheist...

my brother's childhood face sneaks through
his middle aged costume
shouting *trick or treat* *trick or treat*
in the windowless room...
death disguised as a salesman
shows us a price list
gravediggers come up...i'm
transported to Hamlet
scene with the skull
my mother's in my hand for a moment/
too long...

downstairs we must choose:
all kinds of wood
unfinished shiny expensive
huge locks it would take
several men to open
light blue pillow w/white ruffles
too comfortable looking
we pick something suitable
within financial means...
doesn't matter what price they charge
nothing is affordable...

two days from now
Halloween for real

V.

NOT ALL THERE &
HOPE I NEVER WILL BE

can't find me here
          i'm there
when you look
            somewhere
you aren't
           and shouldn't be
            too long
if you're truly human
not programmed everybody
           all there
all the time

GOTTA SEE TO HEAR

ya gotta see to hear
the beat drive fingers across keys
the way it moves in the skin
how a body leans over a piano
a sax speaks in a man's moves
see the trumpet
mute a shout

in the eyes
it's in the eyes

sometimes
ya gotta see
Jackie Byard's funny/silent
laugh to hear his sound
the way Clapton holds his girl
to hear him sweet talk the notes
watch someone pull strings to fly
against the inanimate

speak to me
speak to me

and yes
there it is/& it does
sometimes ya gotta see the one
holding the horn
holds him give
life to what gives
life back   gotta see
birth of sound to hear
with your eyes
when there's no sound at all
and it's the moment   before afterwards
they're jivin
really jivin

A NOD TO DYLAN THOMAS

give 'em hell, i think/hearing
that my mother socked the head
nurse trying to tie her down
when she got up to walk out
of old age's death
screamed for the police/attack dogs...
i was at a memorial
for a street singer last
of the troubadour poets
child of his spirit, among others
eulogizing a guy who raised his own hell

against the Goddamn dead
...that rule this world

i wanted to see this woman/my mother
who lived in a corner of
her life bent over an
ironing board a stove gave
love the only way she knew:
heated up & served
disappointed by what she got back
break free, do what she never dared
wanted her to know just as much,
i couldn't give what hadn't been given
and resented both equally now;
but when i heard what she
did in that hospital
i cheered her on:
i am child of her spirit
as much as his
socking it to death in every poem:

hey jack, it isn't only the dead
the children too rule

**reference to the poet & quote (in ital) is to Jack Micheline*

BLUES TO TONY MOFFEIT ON HEARING OF HERBERT HUNCKE'S DEATH

8/9/96

hey tony...another wordman/outlaw dead...
have you heard?

days before wailing
out of colorado
across the rockies/east
your SOS
blues for kerouac
for the beat
the "jumpin" nights of then...

hey tony...in your frantic wordblast
did you hear

SOS for what isn't anymore
blew into my ear
soft and loud and crazy
SOS i didn't hear till
news of huncke's death tolled
thru your blues
SOS for the hustlers and thieves
who gave back
more than they took...
hipsterghosts
not us
whispering in kid's ears
not us
urging them on

digging up kerouac's bones
again
and again...

blew wild improvs all
week the republican stormtroopers
marched thru the house
thru all our houses...
did you hear them?
in a country founded by outlaws
hunting them down

hey tony...what are we gonna do
        when the last one goes
when there's no one riding into town
        anarchy in his brain
        notebook in pocket...

who will jump start the breath
when there's no ginsberg to remind us

        can we ever
        as fearlessly?

all night blew into my veins
    SOS blues   for kerouac
                                        for us all

POEM FOR AMERICA'S UNOFFICIAL POET LAUREATE

he came to pay homage   Whitman's unnatural first born
been ill   couldn't focus   on/off with his glasses
searching for words left
in a California supermarket long ago
stumbled on now...
we held our breath
prayed he'd make it thru   yes   once more
          be who he was...

his hand weighed down by the book
i gave him to sign

        voice badgering
                  please howl
          i never heard you howl
                              again   please

I am not a performing dog   he howled...

        he was there for Whitman
        we for him
        a difficult evening...

in business suit   frameless glasses
could have been that rebel's father/
we kept looking for him at readings
hoped to hear   and sometimes
in that weary old man's voice
that brash kid who
went to Dr. Williams with this poems
                              that legendary cry...

I never met the man **really** met him
too old   not old enough
for student or contemporary
heterosexual at that
I came late to what he   & they   were about
          all the way when i did...

learned he was dying from a daily tabloid
read it on a crowded no. 5 subway:
                                        right then knew
something major was going down
                                        with the century

. . . .

                                        went down
next day flashed over 42nd street
                radio/tv internet
NY Times LA Times times everywhere
Time magazine the poet laid to rest in Berkeley 1956
        time must acknowledge

first thought best thought
recorded shock: the Poet is gone
                next day
                  gone
                next day
                  gone...

. . . .

voice out of 1950's San Francisco...

what do you mean by naked?

                                        replying
took off his clothes
walked naked thru poems for more than 40 years
first in a century answered Whitman's call:

to those unborn...
Poets to come
...a new brood...
            greater than
            before known
Arouse/For you must justify me

he did singing America's song
to keep those breathing alive poetry alive
ridding language of bullshit
knocked down skeletons in their flesh...
pulitzer/grant committees ignored him
awarded those who never made a sound...
one official laureate's voice with different names/

sang past his critics
louder he had to...

if the man sometimes failed to
live up to the poet's vision
wasn't always as wise
enjoyed his rock star status more
than we thought he should
wasn't always the person who wrote the poems
not every poem soaring lately

isn't it enough he widened the road
wanted America to be better
all of us better...

I enter your secret places with my mind, I speak
with your presence
I roar your lion roar with mortal mouth ....

enough Whitman's child acknowledged his legacy
called out the same:

This ode to you 0 Poets and Orators to come, you father
Whitman as
l join your side, you congress and American people...

called out
next day
calling out
calling out

* Wait Whitman quote from *Poets to come*
* Allen Ginsberg quote from *Plutonian Ode*

BECAUSE YOU CAN'T I WILL

write the poem about all the nannies
in this Brooklyn neighborhood we
lived in mine not yours
the hood missing Bronx edge
you grew up in
raised three kids
made-it -relief after each
wiping plenty of ass sometimes
punching fists thru walls
to get thru ...
Vietnam marriage jobs...
cleaned up your own shit

no wonder you were so struck
by these nannies walked
uneasily thru this safe zone
looking over your shoulder
quick draw eyes on the ready/
feared losing that edge
becoming too sure...

this is the poem you walked away from
the woman who wanted you to stop smoking
drawn to your pall mall breath
to give up: the
spirit that flew you to her
and took you away:

this is the world you couldn't afford

VOICES OF CHERRY VALLEY

For Charles Plymell & the gang
(8/7—8/9/98)

Whitman's road opening freedom's song
roads howling 30 years
3 days sang thru the valley...

old parched road
rumored bank robberies   cold
prison bars   a Kerouac road
rambling thru America
tripping: oranges dancing
w/sunflowers from guitar strings
in the luminous dust
                                        escaped
thru Mississippi mud / road
squeezed out of gut-wrenching
New Orleans   sweated
rain pounding blues
wailing into the earth
unlearning: deeper inside
road that leaves the roads behind
i hitched onto
                                        outside time
cool Wichita
dug out of a hole in the wall
jazz joint moved thru
snapping his   fingers

road fleeing out of control
long green scarf flying around it
operatic roller coaster road
i didn't want to be on
blows itself out

and Wichita
wearing a bandanna
leaning on a stick
keeping realtime   onlytime

sound made of movement
that was sound never stopped

New York road
brick & steel dirt
working man's beer road
taking me for a spin
around town singing *i am*
the old days
                thru
Ginsberg's farm   roadside diners
backcountry roads
daisy roads
roads that made no sense
nobody knew where they began
were heading but
felt good being on
calling out in husky Spanish
I didn't understand
speaking to my blood
with the beat & the sound
new roads i couldn't see
springing up underfoot / alive
with every road...
                        train
chugging thru the valley / whole century
Wichita jumping on   hoping cars

i am the old days

turning in the wheels
Wichita snapping his fingers
   tripping:
                vision 21

FAREWELL TO A DOWNTRODDEN SAINT

—2/27/98

i don't much like this age
hankering after puritan taboos
holy/holier than thou
about everything
hail & brimstone Cotton Mathers
running my city, country
anything alive, x-rated
holy art not exempt either...

walk down any street & see
people huddled in doorways sneaking
a drag, scared criminal by
new morality: in the name of health, family
someone killed, a building blown up;
doesn't matter what we call it now...

nabbed for jay walking
refusing to keep within the lines
overstepping like a child who
doesn't see a line
crayoned red over a coloring book picture
& called into the principal's office
to explain what i couldn't
can't still...breathe between lines
i don't see: *do not step*
on the grass dance on the grass
like a child doesn't know
how to put herself in
a prison, child with young
or old skin who knows in
the scheme of things/no scheme: